FRANCIS FRITH'S

DUNMOW, THAXTED & FINCHINGFIELD

PHOTOGRAPHIC MEMORIES

RUSSELL THOMPSON was born in Chelmsford in 1965 and educated at the town's Grammar School. He currently works in adult education as a creative writing tutor. When not teaching, he is a regular performer on the cabaret and spoken-word circuits, and has recently completed a show at the Edinburgh Festival. Essex, however, is his first love.

Being unmarried, he is not eligible to apply for the Dunmow Flitch.

FRANCIS FRITH'S
PHOTOGRAPHIC MEMORIES

DUNMOW, THAXTED & FINCHINGFIELD

PHOTOGRAPHIC MEMORIES

RUSSELL THOMPSON

First published in the United Kingdom in 2004 by
Frith Book Company Ltd

Limited Hardback Subscribers Edition 2004
ISBN 1-85937-818-8

Paperback Edition 2004
ISBN 1-85937-819-6

British Library Cataloguing in Publication Data

Francis Frith's Dunmow, Thaxted & Finchingfield - Photographic Memories
Russell Thompson

Frith Book Company Ltd
Frith's Barn, Teffont,
Salisbury, Wiltshire SP3 5QP
Tel: +44 (0) 1722 716 376
Email: info@francisfrith.co.uk
www.francisfrith.co.uk

Printed and bound in Great Britain

Front Cover: **GREAT DUNMOW,** *The Market Place & Town Hall
c1955* D90005
Frontispiece: **GREAT DUNMOW,** *High Street c1955* D90002

*The colour-tinting is for illustrative purposes only, and is not intended to
be historically accurate*

The following images of the Frith Trials were supplied by Mike Perry, of David Lipson
Photography:- D90701 (p.14), D90702 (p.15), D90703 (p.15), D90704 (p.16),
D90705 (p.17), D90706 (p.18).

AS WITH ANY HISTORICAL DATABASE THE FRITH ARCHIVE IS
CONSTANTLY BEING CORRECTED AND IMPROVED AND THE
PUBLISHERS WOULD WELCOME INFORMATION ON OMISSIONS
OR INACCURACIES

CONTENTS

ACKNOWLEDGMENTS
The author would like to acknowledge the help of Cecil Ludar-Smith,
Keith & Jean Sutton, Steve & Pat Schorah, Russell Brighton, Bob Gray,
Douglas May and Mike Perry in the writing of this book.

FRANCIS FRITH
VICTORIAN PIONEER

FRANCIS FRITH, founder of the world-famous photographic archive, was a complex and multi-talented man. A devout Quaker and a highly successful Victorian businessman, he was philosophical by nature and pioneering in outlook.

By 1855 he had already established a wholesale grocery business in Liverpool, and sold it for the astonishing sum of £200,000, which is the equivalent today of over £15,000,000. Now a very rich man, he was able to indulge his passion for travel. As a child he had pored over travel books written by early explorers, and his fancy and imagination had been stirred by family holidays to the sublime mountain regions of Wales and Scotland. 'What lands of spirit-stirring and enriching scenes and places!' he had written. He was to return to these scenes of grandeur in later years to 'recapture the thousands of vivid and tender memories', but with a different purpose. Now in his thirties, and captivated by the new science of photography, Frith set out on a series of pioneering journeys up the Nile and to the Near East that occupied him from 1856 until 1860.

INTRIGUE AND EXPLORATION

These far-flung journeys were packed with intrigue and adventure. In his life story, written when he was sixty-three, Frith tells of being held captive by bandits, and of fighting 'an awful midnight battle to the very point of surrender with a deadly pack of hungry, wild dogs'. Wearing flowing Arab costume, Frith arrived at Akaba by camel sixty years before Lawrence of Arabia, where he encountered 'desert princes and rival sheikhs, blazing with jewel-hilted swords'.

He was the first photographer to venture beyond the sixth cataract of the Nile. Africa was still the mysterious 'Dark Continent', and Stanley and Livingstone's historic meeting was a decade into the future. The conditions for picture taking confound belief. He laboured for hours in his wicker dark-room in the sweltering heat of the desert, while the volatile chemicals fizzed dangerously in their trays. Back in London he exhibited his photographs and was 'rapturously cheered' by members of the Royal Society. His reputation as a photographer was made overnight.

VENTURE OF A LIFE-TIME

Characteristically, Frith quickly spotted the opportunity to create a new business as a specialist publisher of photographs. He lived in an era of immense and sometimes violent change.

For the poor in the early part of Victoria's reign work was exhausting and the hours long, and people had precious little free time to enjoy themselves. Most had no transport other than a cart or gig at their disposal, and rarely travelled far beyond the boundaries of their own town or village. However, by the 1870s the railways had threaded their way across the country, and Bank Holidays and half-day Saturdays had been made obligatory by Act of Parliament. All of a sudden the working man and his family were able to enjoy days out and see a little more of the world.

With typical business acumen, Francis Frith foresaw that these new tourists would enjoy having souvenirs to commemorate their days out. In 1860 he married Mary Ann Rosling and set out on a new career: his aim was to photograph every city, town and village in Britain. For the next thirty years he travelled the country by train and by pony and trap, producing fine photographs of seaside resorts and beauty spots that were keenly bought by millions of Victorians. These prints were painstakingly pasted into family albums and pored over during the dark nights of winter, rekindling precious memories of summer excursions.

THE RISE OF FRITH & CO

Frith's studio was soon supplying retail shops all over the country. To meet the demand he gathered about him a small team of photographers, and published the work of independent artist-photographers of the calibre of Roger Fenton and Francis Bedford. In order to gain some understanding of the scale of Frith's business one only has to look at the catalogue issued by Frith & Co in 1886: it runs to some 670 pages, listing not only many thousands of views of the British Isles but also many photographs of most European countries, and China, Japan, the USA and Canada - note the sample page shown on page 9 from the hand-written Frith & Co ledgers recording the pictures. By 1890 Frith had created the greatest specialist photographic publishing company in the world, with over 2,000 sales outlets - more than the combined number that Boots and WH Smith have today! The picture on the next page shows the Frith & Co display board at Ingleton in the Yorkshire Dales (left of window). Beautifully constructed with a mahogany frame and gilt inserts, it could display up to a dozen local scenes.

POSTCARD BONANZA

The ever-popular holiday postcard we know today took many years to develop. In 1870 the Post Office issued the first plain cards, with a pre-printed stamp on one face. In 1894 they allowed other publishers' cards to be sent through the mail with an attached adhesive halfpenny stamp. Demand grew rapidly, and in 1895 a new size of postcard was permitted called the court card, but there was little room for illustration. In 1899, a year after Frith's death, a new card measuring 5.5 x 3.5 inches became the standard format, but it was not until 1902 that the divided back came into being, so that the address and message could be on one face and a full-size illustration on the other. Frith & Co were in the vanguard of postcard development: Frith's sons Eustace and Cyril continued their father's monumental task, expanding the number of views offered to the public and recording more and more places in Britain, as the coasts and countryside were opened up to mass travel.

Francis Frith had died in 1898 at his villa in Cannes, his great project still growing. The archive he created continued in business for another seventy years. By 1970 it contained over a third of a million pictures showing 7,000 British towns and villages.

FRANCIS FRITH'S LEGACY

Frith's legacy to us today is of immense significance and value, for the magnificent archive of evocative photographs he created provides a unique record of change in the cities, towns and villages throughout Britain over a century and more. Frith and his fellow studio photographers revisited locations many times down the years to update their views, compiling for us an enthralling and colourful pageant of British life and character.

We are fortunate that Frith was dedicated to recording the minutiae of everyday life. For it is this sheer wealth of visual data, the painstaking chronicle of changes in dress, transport, street layouts, buildings, housing, engineering and landscape that captivates us so much today. His remarkable images offer us a powerful link with the past and with the lives of our ancestors.

THE VALUE OF THE ARCHIVE TODAY

Computers have now made it possible for Frith's many thousands of images to be accessed almost instantly. Frith's images are increasingly used as visual resources, by social historians, by researchers into genealogy and ancestry, by architects and town planners, and by teachers involved in local history projects.

In addition, the archive offers every one of us an opportunity to examine the places where we and our families have lived and worked down the years. Highly successful in Frith's own era, the archive is now, a century and more on, entering a new phase of popularity. Historians consider the Francis Frith Collection to be of prime national importance. It is the only archive of its kind remaining in private ownership. Francis Frith's archive is now housed in an historic timber barn in the beautiful village of Teffont in Wiltshire. Its founder would not recognize the archive office as it is today. In place of the many thousands of dusty boxes containing glass plate negatives and an all-pervading odour of photographic chemicals, there are now ranks of computer screens. He would be amazed to watch his images travelling round the world at unimaginable speeds through internet lines.

The archive's future is both bright and exciting. Francis Frith, with his unshakeable belief in making photographs available to the greatest number of people, would undoubtedly approve of what is being done today with his lifetime's work. His photographs depicting our shared past are now bringing pleasure and enlightenment to millions around the world a century and more after his death.

DUNMOW, THAXTED
& FINCHINGFIELD
AN INTRODUCTION

ONE DAY, towards the end of the Great War, a man stood in a North Essex church peering up at his handiwork. There above him hung the flags of the Allies, the flag of St George, and a couple of others. These were dark days, and the man suspected that there would be other dark days to come. However, he was not without his beliefs: he believed in God - a sociable, fair-minded God who enjoyed singing and dancing and playing party games - and he believed in the latest flag that he had hung in the church. It was pure red - red like poppies, red as the Essex shield.

The third thing that the Rev Conrad Noel believed in was his parish - although it was a curiously remote one for south-east England, and was centred on a decayed industrial town. But Thaxted was beginning to re-invent itself: it had a hat factory and a small sweet factory, and things were looking up.

And Conrad Noel, staunch Christian Socialist, had recently made a new friend. The composer Gustav Holst had fallen in love with Thaxted a few years previously, and was currently ensconced in a house just below the church. It was only a matter of time before he turned up and offered to help with the choir. So deep was Holst's love, that he named a tune after the place: that setting for *I Vow To Thee My Country*,

THAXTED, *The Post Office 1906* 55463

which crops up in *The Planets*, and which recently became something of a rugby anthem, is called *Thaxted*.

Thaxted's near neighbours Finchingfield and Great Dunmow also have their little niches in our popular culture. Finchingfield has appeared on so many calendars and table-mats, that it has a universal currency: nearly everyone recognises it on some level or another. And Dunmow? Well, Dunmow has its Flitch.

Like the Campden Wonder or the Winnersh Triangle, the Dunmow Flitch is something that many people are vaguely aware of, even if they are not quite sure what it is. What it is is this: an ancient custom whereby a flitch of bacon - a whole side of a pig - is presented to a married couple who have not, in the past 366 days, 'offended each other in deed or in word' nor in any way regretted their marriage. If this sounds solemn, it was originally intended to do so. The process seems to have been instigated by the church as a means of underlining the sanctity of wedlock. Similar customs equating bacon and fertility have survived in other corners of Europe.

At Dunmow, the award was made by the authorities of Little Dunmow Priory. At the Dissolution, this prerogative passed to the lord of the manor. Claimants had to swear an oath whilst kneeling on a pair of long-vanished sharp stones. Up until 1751, we only have six documented instances of the Flitch being won, but the ceremony was far better-known than such statistics suggest. Langland mentions it in *The Vision of Piers Plowman*, Chaucer in *The Wife of Bath's Tale*. It evidently drew the crowds.

Despite - or because of - its popularity, the Flitch was allowed to lapse for a hundred years.

Prospective claimants would find the manor gates nailed shut. In 1855, though, the prolific novelist William Harrison Ainsworth revived the custom on the back of his book *The Flitch of Bacon*. He was not a man to shy away from self-publicity, and appointed himself as a sort of 'special guest star' at the festivities. Ainsworth initiated many changes - most importantly, the relocation of the ceremony to Great Dunmow. Moral guardians saw the new Flitch as a travesty - it was accompanied by music, junketing and mass shop-closure - but really it had been heading that way ever since the suppression of the Priory.

The revival gathered momentum in the latter half of the 19th century, though some of the occasions were farcically mismanaged. Nonetheless, it seemed as if the custom was back to stay. Now known as the Dunmow Flitch Trials, the new ceremony involved tongue-in-cheek court officials and a jury of 'six maidens and six bachelors'. The two World Wars interrupted the fun, but the Flitch has now settled down as a four-yearly event, the next being in July 2004. Interested parties are invited to peruse www.dunmowflitchtrials.co.uk - a far cry, indeed, from those two sharp stones.

Great Dunmow is justly proud of its Flitch, but it is important to remember that it is also a living, working town with its own long history. It developed from a Roman station at the intersection of two long, straight roads. Its market - granted in 1253 - was a busy conduit for the livestock, corn and dairy goods being produced by the area's farms. As with many other Essex towns, however, much of Dunmow's prosperity was to come with the influx of Flemish weavers at the end of the 16th century. When the local cloth trade fizzled out, the town became more reliant on other industries, such as brewing. It is significant that its excellent little museum is housed in the former maltings in Mill Lane. Today, Dunmow is an active, concentrated town with a strong sense of community - and also a sense of not having got too big for itself.

Thaxted lies seven miles north of Dunmow, on one of those Roman roads. A settlement sprang up, in Saxon times if not before, where the road crossed a small tributary of the Chelmer. Thaxted's future was then wide open, and it has been said that had circumstances been different, it might have become 'another Sheffield'. It was the Earls of Clare, the lords of the manor, who introduced a cutlery industry here. It boomed, and the cutlers soon became the dominant force in the parish. At the end of the 14th century they threw up a Guildhall from which they could govern their town. Behind it was a colossal church, still only half-built then. By the time Thaxted achieved borough status in 1556, however, the cutlery business was on its way out. As at Dunmow, there had also been a

cloth trade here for some time, and to some extent it slowed down the economic slump that finally hit Thaxted in earnest. Phases of agricultural hardship did not help, and by the mid-19th century, the town was 'languishing for lack of railway communication' as well.

Noel, Holst, and Noel's successor Jack Putterill set the cultural tone for Thaxted in the 20th century. One contemporary recalls seeing the town full of 'odd-looking men in sandals and women in hand-woven costumes', though the description was not unkindly meant. The longed-for railway came and went. But by then, Thaxted had grown reasonably self-supporting and - more importantly - had rediscovered its own worth.

Travel east from Thaxted, and you come to Finchingfield, a village at the mercy of its own image. For centuries it had developed in an unremarked-on, villagey way. Then, quite early in the 20th century, with the dissemination of photography, Finchingfield suddenly became quaint. The internal combustion engine completed the equation, and Finchingfield now

FINCHINGFIELD, *Haverhill Road c1960* F77037

swarms with day trippers in the summer months. It is, in the words of one resident, 'like Torremolinos'. Litter is a problem, and so is parking. The population - hovering around the 1,000 mark - largely consists of London commuters. Not that it is so different from several other North Essex villages in that respect, although many people obviously bemoan the breakdown of the old-style rural community.

Some of Finchingfield's visitors, apparently, are not wholly sure what to do once they get there - for there is little here besides the church, the windmill, the antiques centre and the view. This is Finchingfield's trump card: 'What you see is what you get', it seems to say.

The adjacent villages of Wethersfield and Great Bardfield are both, in their way, mini-Finchingfields; but they are not tourist destinations. Wethersfield, in particular, is a satisfyingly quiet backwater. So, for that matter, are Stebbing and Debden, and most of the other places in this book.

All these towns and villages share a common geography and a common past: they share a rolling, clayey landscape and a history built on weaving, agriculture and straw-plaiting. They are united, too, by the shadow of a common future. At the end of 2003, the Transport Secretary gave the green light to the expansion of Stansted Airport. This would mean the loss of 1,750 acres of farmland and of roughly a hundred homes - including 27 listed buildings and two heritage sites. Hatfield Forest would be seriously threatened by the increased pollution; the much-admired gardens of Easton Lodge would

close. Of the places in this book, Takeley, Great Easton and, most of all, Bamber's Green are in the greatest danger.

Essex is close to London and full of open space. These blessings become a curse whenever airports are mooted. So what is the answer? As with most transport issues, the problem lies in the attitudes of our society: too many people are too reliant on foreign travel. It is Finchingfield on a global scale. Even bearing this in mind, though, the anti-airport lobby still claims that the new proposals are unnecessary, and has vowed to pursue the matter through the legal system. Stansted's new perimeter fence would come within three miles of Great Dunmow. For a town whose reputation rests on the promotion of human harmony, it is grimly ironic.

Back in the 1920s, the ecclesiastical court ordered Conrad Noel to take down his red flag from Thaxted church. It had already been torn down and reinstated on a number of occasions. He must realise, they said, that even the strongest political fervour must ultimately acknowledge a higher authority. Noel bit his famous hare-lip until the following Sunday, and then declared from the pulpit that 'the flag has been removed, but the preaching will go on.'

The red flag can also be a symbol of peril. It depends on the context. At the start of the 21st century, Noel's church is still pretty much as he left it. It is a well known landmark; and well known, too, to pilots, who use it for lining-up their approach to Stansted's runway. It is not, at the time of writing, a particularly happy ending.

Then again, perhaps it is not an ending at all.

THE FLITCH TRIALS

GREAT DUNMOW
The Flitch Trials, Courtroom Scene 2000
D90701

Here we see the Judge - solicitor Michael Chapman - assessing the claims of the vying couples. Claimants are quizzed on various aspects of their nuptial harmony. Prior to the custom's 1851 revival, the court was presided over by the steward of the manor of Little Dunmow.

GREAT DUNMOW
The Flitch Trials, Leading Counsel Claire Rayner 2000 D90702

Agony aunt Claire Rayner has been a long-term fixture of the trials in her role as Leading Counsel. Although well known for her waggish mode of cross-examination, she says that 'It's not just good fun, but it shows that marriage really matters.' This, indeed, harks back to the ceremony's original function.

GREAT DUNMOW, *The Flitch Trials, the Jury and the Court Usher 2000* D90703

It seems that the custom first acquired a jury in 1701, when it was composed of five young ladies: the four daughters of the lord of the manor, and the steward's one daughter. The jurors' unmarried status is supposed to give them an untainted view of married life. Three of the people in this picture are allegedly vegetarians.

GREAT DUNMOW
The Flitch Trials, Taking the Oath 2000 D90704

The Rev Keith Holloway is reading the oath at the top of Star Lane. This is a rousing piece of verse insisting that the claimants have not engaged in 'Household Brawls or Contentious Strife' or wished to be 'unmarried again'. The words are first quoted in Thomas Fuller's 1662 book *Worthies of England*.

GREAT DUNMOW
The Flitch Trials, Chairing the Winners 2000 D90705

In 2000 the flitch was awarded to four couples. This is Fred and
Joan Shepherd (themselves Dunmow residents) being carried in a
replica of the ancient Flitch Chair. The original item - a hotch-
potch of medieval woodwork from Dunmow Priory - is kept
securely in Little Dunmow church. The replica lives in the
museum at the Maltings.

GREAT DUNMOW
The Flitch Trials, the Flitch itself 2000 D90706

Central to the ceremony is the flitch of bacon itself. Here it is, hung from a frame and draped with greenery. For much of the 20th century, the flitches were supplied by Dunmow's own bacon factory, which occupied a site near the now-vanished railway station. Since the factory's closure in 1984, the ceremony has luckily found new sponsorship.

These photographs of the Flitch Trials were taken by Mike Perry, of David Lipson Photography, who has actually won the Flitch himself.

GREAT AND LITTLE DUNMOW

LITTLE DUNMOW
Priory Place c1955 L155001

The Dunmow Flitch began as an ecclesiastical ceremony connected with Dunmow Priory. Nothing remains of the priory itself (other than its chapel and the indents left by its fishponds), but this house overlies part of the site. Once divided into four, it has now been knocked into one property again. It is at least 17th-century, if not older.

LITTLE DUNMOW
The Street c1955
L155002

When the Flitch ceremony still took place in Little Dunmow, successful claimants were paraded through the village in the Flitch Chair. The ceremonial bacon itself was carried in front, on a pole. Little Dunmow's pub, itself named The Flitch of Bacon, is the last building visible here in the distance.

GREAT DUNMOW
Braintree Road c1955 D90033

The bus in the distance has just passed Ford Bridge. Once called Stratford (the 'street ford'), this was where the Roman road crossed the River Chelmer. In the distance are the trees of Merks Hill - itself a known site of Roman habitation - and on our left is the ribbon development that had started creeping along this road in the 1920s.

GREAT DUNMOW, *High Street c1965* D90059

This is the High Street's southern end. Stokes the butcher's (right) still has the wooden sign on its roof to this day. Saracen's Cottage (far left) once accommodated servants and horses whilst their superiors were staying at The Saracen's Head, Dunmow's main coaching-inn. The flail, tun and wheatsheaf plastered on its façade represent the town's former sources of livelihood.

GREAT DUNMOW
High Street c1960
D90030

The shop with the Senior Service canopies (right) belonged to Dorothy 'Dolly' Dowsett. She sold sweets, stationery, records, toys, ice cream, and the ever-popular 'fancy goods'. She remained in business until 1973. Next door was Rumsey's carpet and bedding shop, and beyond that, the long frontage of the Eastern Electricity showroom.

GREAT DUNMOW
High Street c1965
D90060

The house on the left - The Gables - was the home and office of the solicitor Frederick Snell (who died in 1900). The practice was taken over by Albert Floyd, whose partners kept the firm going until 1968. It is still a solicitor's today. The bowed frontage next door was once the shop of William Stacey, florist and photographer.

GREAT DUNMOW, *High Street c1955* D90010

Dunmow's post office has been in the red brick building (centre) since 1939. A barn, used for meetings by local dissenters, once stood on the site. The three-storey White House next door was home to Dunmow Rural District Council from 1934 until 1974, when it was swallowed by Uttlesford District Council. It is still used by Uttlesford as Community Information offices.

GREAT DUNMOW
New Street c1965
D90072

Tucked behind the White House, New Street has always been a residential quarter. It already had its name in 1419. The street remains largely unchanged, though the cottage on the right has recently undergone a thorough restoration. The shop at the street's left-hand corner was once Legg's bakery; it is now Wilden's Restaurant.

GREAT DUNMOW
High Street c1955
D90002

Several of these shop
fronts have swapped
their identities. The
three-dormered roof
(centre left) belongs to
what was, in 1955, The
White Horse. The
canopied shop where the
road bends (centre) is
one of Dunmow's recent
cornerstones: May &
Brett's newsagent and
bookshop (established
1935 by Basil May and
now run by his grandsons
Nigel and Julian).

GREAT DUNMOW
The Town Hall
c1955 D90001

Barclay's Bank (right,
now Hetherington's
estate agents) replaced
an old shop that
variously served as a
confectioner's and a
butcher's. Prints of the
1855 Flitch procession
show throngs of
spectators hanging out
of the building's
windows. Between the
taking of this
photograph and No
D90062 on page 26,
Barclay's acquired an
extra storey.

GREAT DUNMOW
High Street c1965
D90062

The four pointed gables were built in 1899 on the site of two small cottages and a plastered building that seemed to be the remainder of an ancient chapel. The left-hand shop of the pair is now occupied by the long-established chemist Roper's, though at the time of our photograph it belonged to the builder's merchants Brown & Son.

GREAT DUNMOW
High Street c1960
D90043

Although under different management, Arthur Willett's shop (left) still bears his name. He opened the premises in 1896 as a newsagent-cum-hairdresser. He was also a photographer - his studio was in the summerhouse of a garden in White Street. The shop branched out, at various times, into making umbrellas and selling musical instruments.

GREAT DUNMOW, *Stortford Road c1955* D90020

The Georgian façade of the Saracen's Head masks a 17th-century pub. It was an important staging-post, and it has hosted numerous celebrations, meetings, balls and auctions at key points in Dunmow's history (such as the banquet to mark the coming of the railway). The annual parish dinners were held here in the 19th century.

GREAT DUNMOW
Stortford Road c1960
D90046

'This is Jason's Supplies' says the hand-written sign in the window (left). Supplying what, exactly? It is now Happy Happy Garden, a Chinese takeaway. The area behind this row of buildings - bounded by The Chequers (with the tall chimneys, centre left) and The Saracen's Head in the High Street - was once the site of a market dealing in cattle, corn and poultry.

GREAT DUNMOW, *The Chequers, Stortford Road c1955* D90024

It would seem to be Dunmow's Carnival week, judging by the banner strung from the Chequers. On the left, with the tubs of foliage, stands the oldest-established butcher's in the town. Formerly Lucking's, it was taken over by John Sweetland in 1950. The house on the extreme left now contains Uttlesford Voluntary Services.

GREAT DUNMOW
The Market Place and the Town Hall c1955
D90005

Originally built in the 1570s, the Town Hall has been renovated several times. The bell in the turret used to double as market-bell and fire-bell. When the Flitch ceremony was resurrected in the 19th century, the claimants underwent their mock trials in the Town Hall; and it was where the Dunmow Corporation met until being abolished in 1888.

GREAT DUNMOW
Market Place
c1960 D90042

The International
Stores (right) - 'grocers
and tea-dealers' - were
a sort of early chain
store. Banana Travel is
there now. Next door
is the four-gabled
frontage of Thomas
Pannell's fishmonger's
shop. By the mid
1960s, Dunmow's
electric cables were
being put
underground: our
photo shows what a
good thing this was,
aesthetically speaking.

GREAT DUNMOW
Market Place c1965
D90056

This innocuous-looking
road-junction was the
backdrop for
Dunmow's pump riot of
1786. The authorities
removed the pump that
stood here, only to have
it re-installed by the
townspeople. This
happened more than
once. The affair finally
escalated into a full-
scale fight, which ended
with twelve pro-pump
protesters being thrown
into Chelmsford Gaol.

GREAT DUNMOW
Market Place c1965
D90055

Lewis's (left) has a fine array of braziers, bins and barrows outside. This was an old-fashioned ironmonger's that kept its nails and screws in small drawers behind the counter. The Brooke Bond van outside is presumably visiting the adjacent grocer's, Luckin & Sons. This shop still has the family name up, though it currently seems to be full of soft toys.

GREAT DUNMOW
Market Place c1965 D90068

Mr Collier's shop (left), with its cheerful assortment of Lyons Maid, Woodbines and footballs, is still fondly remembered. The dark carriageway beside the Kiwi Café, next door, was formerly the entrance to the Crown Brewery. Established here in 1866, the premises were auctioned-off 105 years later.

GREAT DUNMOW
Doctor's Pond c1965
D90067

Older than the Crown Brewery, Dunmow Brewery had 18th-century origins. The main structure - seen here - dated from 1834. It owned several pubs, and produced its own beers, such as Blue Boar Brown and Double Dunmow. In 1965 it was bought-up by Charrington's. The site ran to seed before being redeveloped as the Maltings estate in the 1980s.

GREAT DUNMOW, *Doctor's Pond c1965* D90066

The Brick House (centre) is all that remains of Dunmow Brewery. Facing it across the road (right) was Wilson's bakery. This was previously owned by Frank Coates (dubbed 'Coates the Pond' to distinguish him from Fred Coates, the baker at Church End). Wilson's ceased trading in the mid 1990s, and is now a private house.

GREAT DUNMOW
The Downs c1960
D90054

The Downs is a large, undulating green next to Doctor's Pond. This is a detached portion, looking towards Rosemary Avenue. Rosemary Lane, behind us, used to be known as Windmill Street, because of the mill that once lurked behind this row of houses. Part of the Downs, Talberds Ley, plays host to the Flitch festivities.

GREAT DUNMOW
The Downs
c1955 D90007

Doctor's Pond takes its name from a Dr John Raynor (d 1804), a local surgeon who kept it supplied with fish. It is better known, however, for its connections with a contemporary of his: Lionel Lukin, an upmarket coach-builder, invented the first 'unsinkable' lifeboat, and experimented with prototypes on Doctor's Pond in 1785.

GREAT DUNMOW, *Clock House c1960* D90051

Dating from c1580, Clock House had two famous residents. The first, Ann Line, was executed in 1601 for concealing a Catholic priest here. She was canonised in 1970. The second, Sir George Howland Beaumont (1753-1827), was an art collector who effectively founded the National Gallery. He used to entertain the likes of Wordsworth and Coleridge at Clock House.

GREAT DUNMOW
Parsonage Downs
c1955 D90037

Cricketers' Pond takes its name from the pub whose sign is visible in the background (left). The pond often becomes silted up, and has to be dredged by local volunteers. Behind us is the entrance to Dunmow's secondary school, Helena Romanes, which was built in 1958-59 to replace the Council School on the Downs.

GREAT DUNMOW
Parsonage Downs
c1960 D90049

This is the driveway leading to Newton Hall, which was once one of Dunmow's seven outlying manors. It is named in the *Domesday Book*. The first edition of the Ordnance Survey map marks both the Hall and the obelisk standing proudly in its grounds. The grounds are currently being engulfed by the new Woodlands Park estate.

GREAT DUNMOW
Church End c1960
D90041

This view is now partially obscured by a development of old people's homes. The earliest part of the church - the chancel - dates from c1320, the nave and tower from a few decades later. Until the 1540s, much of the church's revenue came from its troupe of resident players, who put on shows at Christmas, May Day and Corpus Christi.

GREAT DUNMOW, *Church End c1955* D90028

Church End was a fairly self-contained community. Its situation, half a mile from the town centre, has prompted a number of hypotheses of the chicken-or-egg variety. The car in the foreground is an Austin Ruby, antiquated even then; the van, one imagines, belongs to the shop - a bakery that is now a decorator's.

GREAT DUNMOW
St Mary's Parish Church c1960 D90048

The sanctus bell, which once hung in the little empty bellcote, was presumably removed at the Reformation. Later, when the religious tables turned, the Catholic vicar John Bird was appointed here. Bishop Bonner once visited Dunmow to see him preach. Bird, however, apparently suffered some sort of breakdown mid-sermon, leaving Bonner squirming with embarrassed indignation.

THAXTED

THAXTED
Town Street from Mill End c1950 T28050

Two windmills once stood at this end of town, hence the name. Beside the clapboarded cottage is Franklin's butcher's shop. This used to get flushed out and cleaned once a week, sending water coursing down the street. Next door is the Co-op drapery. The white house across the road was, until 1908, The Sun - a rival for The Star (opposite).

THAXTED
Town Street c1950
T28014

Under the two awnings on the left are Foster's bakery (advertising Hovis above) and Clunas the chemist (advertising Iron Jelloids). Further down, on the pavement, is the town's pump. Few Essex children were left untouched by the half-hidden smokestack on the right: it belonged to George Lee's sweet factory at Mill End. The works' hooter was a familiar sound in Thaxted.

THAXTED
Town Street c1950
T28013

Frank Barret's garage (left) took over the premises of an Edwardian hat factory. The garage supplied petrol via a long arm that swung out over the pavement, as we can see here. Above the garage was a snooker hall. The tall building two doors along is the 15th-century Recorder's House. Its right-hand neighbour, the Manse, was home to Gustav Holst between 1917 and 1925.

THAXTED
The Guildhall 1906
55458

This is how the Guildhall looked before its 1911 restoration. Allegedly built around the start of the 15th century, this was the headquarters of the Cutlers' Guild, and later the meeting-place of the town's burgesses. Thaxted's craftsmen had slowly wrested the town from manorial control; their Guildhall, symbolically, stood on the site of the manor gates.

THAXTED, *The Guildhall 1951* T28024

In 1910-11 the vicar, Conrad Noel, engaged a furniture restorer called Ernest Beckwith to exercise his skill on restoring the Guildhall. Controversially, he removed the plasterwork - thus exposing the timber-framing - and disposed of the 500-year-old arches between the posts on the ground floor. This photo depicts a later restoration (which included the demolition of a chimney).

THAXTED
The Guildhall c1951 T28055

Thaxted suffered a disastrous fire in 1881: over a hundred people were rendered homeless. The Guildhall's roof caught alight, and several houses in Fishmarket Street (left) were destroyed and never rebuilt. Fishmarket Street was Thaxted's medieval market place. The second cottage on the left is now the library.

THAXTED
Stoney Lane c1955 T28042

This was the original course of the high street. The cluster of timbered houses are of late 15th century date. The one to the left of the pointed gable is called Dick Turpin's Cottage, though it does not have any documented link with the famous thug. The house contains 16th-century wall paintings of plants and birds.

THAXTED
The Post Office 1906
55463

This is an excellent study of an Edwardian post office, with the postman on his cart, the telegraph boys at the door, and the postcards on display. The tree-bark ornamentation of the lintels and window-boxes is an unusual feature. The white house next door - known as The Priory - was a 'ladies' boarding school' at the time of our photograph.

THAXTED
Watling Street c1955
T28015

Everybody here looks comfortably 1950s: the man on the right is wearing his suit even for pushing a wheelbarrow. The Cock (right) was a pub until the 1960s, selling 'beer, spiritous liquors and tobacco', as it still says on a painted fanlight. Traditionally, this was the church-builders' watering-hole of choice. The Co-op (left) was formerly Tanner's grocery and drapery shop.

THAXTED
Bolford Street c1955
T28020

The name of this street signifies a 'bulls' ford' across the Chelmer (which is just a trickle here). Thaxted's great fire of 1881 started here, in a smithy that stood near the telegraph pole. As it happened, Thaxted had had a fire-engine since 1835: one of its homes, the Engine House, is built onto the side of the thatched house (centre).

THAXTED, *Newbiggen Street c1955* T28017

Sherman Ferris's bakery (left) used to stock ice cream, and was therefore much-frequented by children. It also evidently stocked Daren bread - a popular Hovis-like brand in its day. The thatched roofs in the distance are still there, appropriately enough: the town's name means 'place where thatch comes from'.

THAXTED
Newbiggen Street c1955
T28018

Newbiggen ('new building') Street sprang up in response to the town's medieval prosperity. It was once called 'Vikerestrete'. The triple-storeyed house (centre left) is where the Thaxted Morris Ring was constituted in 1934. Their earlier get-togethers, under the tutelage of the Rev Conrad Noel, had taken place at the Coach House, just out of shot on the left.

THAXTED
The Almshouses
1906 55464

These two buildings, the Chantry and the almshouses, stand at the rear of the churchyard. (The sharply-lettered gravestone on the left, incidentally, has now had its epitaph washed away by weather and acid rain.) The Chantry (left) was built as a priest's house. It later served as four almshouses, but it was falling into disrepair by the early 1900s.

THAXTED
The Almshouses
c1955 T28016

In 1933 the Rev Conrad Noel had the Chantry renovated and converted into a single dwelling, owned by the church. The tiled almshouses were modernised in 1975. It has been conjectured that they were built from the timbers of an older building, the Guildhall of St John, which had stood just off Newbiggen Street until the early 18th century.

THAXTED, *The Windmill and the Church c1950* T28041

John Webb, a landowner and publican, constructed this mill in 1804. It ceased its working life in 1910 and has spent the past thirty years undergoing a series of restorations, the most recent of which should be finished in April 2004. The author recently watched the mill's aluminium-covered cap being hoisted off by a crane.

THAXTED
From the West c1955
T28019

This skyline is a useful synopsis of Thaxted: we see a half-rural, half-industrial village, with a cathedral-sized church. Much of the land here was once the grounds of the manor house - the park and the gardens. The prominent feature to the left of the church is the United Reformed Church, built in 1876 to replace an earlier structure.

THAXTED
Clarence House c1960 T28091

Clarence House is now one of Essex County Council's community education centres: it runs such things as residential art courses. The house was built in 1715 - or that, at least, is the date on the rainwater heads. Up to the right runs Bell Lane, named after an ancient inn that has long been given over to other commercial uses.

THAXTED, *The Church from the North-West 1906* 55467

Thaxted once had two churches: one on this site, and one where Rails Farm now stands. The present building was begun in 1340 and completed in 1510. The project was probably part-financed by the Earls of Clare, who owned the manor. The elaborate north porch incorporates a chapel to the 14th-century peasant leader John Ball.

THAXTED, *The Parish Church c1950* T28076

The Swan (left) has an extensive Georgian frontage, nine bays wide. Originally, there were eleven. It once had its own oasthouse and maltings, and a cattle-market used to take place in the inn yard. There are documented references to the 'signum cygni' (the sign of The Swan) as early as the 1540s.

THAXTED, *The Parish Church c1960* T28098

In the time it took to build the church, England went through several architectural styles. The south porch is older and accordingly simpler than the north porch. The medieval church was as high as it was long - but a later miscalculation on the part of some 18th-century restorers left the steeple 2ft shorter than the nave and chancel.

THAXTED
The Church Interior 1906 55468

The most conspicuous feature here is the 15th-century font cover (right). The pulpit, with its sounding-board and slender oak stem (centre right), dates from the 1680s. The church is notable for its sense of spaciousness: the old box-pews were done away with in 1877 and replaced with chairs. A huge iron chandelier now hangs from the central arch.

THAXTED
Bronze Head of the Rev Conrad Noel c1955 T28026

Conrad Noel's incumbency (1910-42) was a colourful time for Thaxted. He was a Socialist, and sometimes upset people with his liberal use of the red flag. He sought to make the church central to Thaxted's social life, embellishing it with the dancers and musicians he invited to perform here. This head was made by the sculptor Gertrude Hermes.

FINCHINGFIELD

FINCHINGFIELD
St John the Baptist's Church 1903 50570

The sturdy Norman tower - reinforced with iron bands - once had a tall, leaded spire, which blew down 'at Cromwell's exit' (in 1658, that is). The clock was only a year old when this picture was taken: it had been fitted in 1902 for Edward VII's coronation. The small obelisk commemorates the wonderfully-named parishioner Swan Tabrum.

FINCHINGFIELD, *Vicarage Lane c1960* F77059

This is the road that leads to the village school. The house in the centre, Cabbaches, proclaims the date 1390 on a plaque near its front door. It is built along medieval lines, with a central hall flanked by a buttery and solar - a provision store and relaxation room respectively.

The Guildhall was built c1500 to house the Trinity Guild, a body formed to find a priest to say Mass. The building was later used to administer the 'benefit, succour and relief of inhabitants of Finchingfield'. It also included almshouses. In recent years, it has been re-jigged to comprise a museum, a library and four self-contained flats.

FINCHINGFIELD, *Church Hill c1965* F77079

Finchingfield church's best-known incumbent was the Puritan preacher Stephen Marshall (c1595-1655), an ungainly man who nevertheless impressed all the right people with his powers of oratory. He had organisational flair, too, and kicked Finchingfield's vestry meetings into shape. After seventeen years here, he was seduced by Parliament's offer to become their parish lecturer, and left for London.

FINCHINGFIELD
The Green c1965 F77075

The house nearest the camera was once the village poorhouse. It dates from the 16th century. There was room for about thirty inmates, who were expected to earn their keep, mainly by spinning. Later the house became a butcher's: older residents recall blood dribbling down into the picturesque village-pond.

FINCHINGFIELD
The Green c1960
F77047

Finchingfield combines a water supply (Finchingfield Brook) with a defensible site (Church Hill). What made sense to Saxon settlers has made it Essex's most photographed village. This has its pros and cons: the narrow bridge looks quaint, but it has to take up to 500 coachloads of visitors a year. And there is no car-park.

FINCHINGFIELD
The Green c1960
F77014

The Fox (left) was owned by the now-defunct Dunmow Brewery. In 1999, the pub became famous for its pet chicken, Violet, who had allegedly been pecking at the war-memorial. The village became split over the matter, and the publican had Violet's life insured. The affair made the newspapers as far away as Australia.

FINCHINGFIELD, *The Green c1960* F77007

Finchingfield's waterfowl are bold creatures, accustomed to this kind of attention. The feeder's headscarf, mid-calf hemline and big collar and cuffs are typical of the period. The tall Georgian building behind her was the Congregational church's manse.

FINCHINGFIELD
The Memorial c1965
F77063

The red brick building in the centre was a day school and lecture hall attached to the 18th-century Congregational church (the white pediment behind it). The school has been converted into a house by the architect Robert Wood. Note the staddle stones around the war memorial: granaries were traditionally built upon these, as rats cannot negotiate them.

FINCHINGFIELD, *Sunnyside House c1960* F77015

When the photograph was taken, this attractive 17th-century house was the headquarters of Wiffen's Coaches Ltd: note the cavernous garages at the rear, and the petrol pump (left). Sunnyside remains intact today (as does the water pump on the green), but the garages have been supplanted by a new road - Coachman's Mead - and, to the right, a new house.

FINCHINGFIELD
The Pond c1965 F77064

The driver of this MG Magnette was perhaps distracted by the vista around him, and has himself become something of a tourist attraction. The building on the bridge (dated 1910) was a grocery shop in the 1960s; it is now a craft-shop, with Olly's Unisex Hair Salon upstairs. Its small annexe is the Hansel und Gretel gift-shop.

FINCHINGFIELD
The Pond c1960
F77021

When cars were rarer here, the village children used to sit on the green and hold sweepstakes, guessing on the number-plate of the next vehicle to pass through. They would have a field day now. This row of cottages pictured is called the Causeway. The dormered Causeway Tea Cottage on the right now offers 'Full Monty' cream teas.

FINCHINGFIELD
Haverhill Road
c1960 F77025

This part of Finchingfield is known as Duck End. The mill lurks behind the attractive cottages in the foreground. It has been said that For Sale signs appear on Finchingfield's most desirable properties whenever bonuses come up in the City.

FINCHINGFIELD
Haverhill Road
c1960 F77036

Finchingfield has the smallest windmill in Essex. It was already here by the 1750s, according to a dated graffito inside. It had stood idle for nearly a hundred years, becoming increasingly dilapidated, when the parish asked Essex County Council to take it in hand in 1957. Now in good condition, it is open every third Sunday during the summer months.

FINCHINGFIELD, *Haverhill Road c1960* F77037

The cottage on our right was formerly a shop. Finchingfield had five provision shops in the first half of the 20th century. It now has only one - the post office. The overgrown watercourse (in the middle of the verge) is a feeder of Finchingfield Brook. The signpost directs us to Spains Hall, a large Elizabethan manor house.

THE SURROUNDING VILLAGES: NORTH

WETHERSFIELD
Church of St Mary Magdalene 1903
50572

At the time of writing, the church is undergoing a major restoration. The stumpy tower dates from around 1200. It used to be taller, but had its upper stage removed in the 17th century. The young Patrick Brontë came here as a curate in 1806. What classics would his brood have produced had they grown up here, rather than at Haworth?

WETHERSFIELD
Silver Street c1965
W192002

The property on the extreme left was previously Mr Baines's shop: he was a grocer and draper, and also sold such things as liquid paraffin. In the early 1950s the bow-windowed house across the road was one of the few to have a television: half of Wethersfield flocked there to watch the Coronation.

WETHERSFIELD
The Green 1903 50571

In this picture, Baines's (in the distance, left) was still flourishing. Like Finchingfield, this village is based around a triangular green - though Wethersfield's is smaller than it once was, owing to road widening. During the Second World War, there was an encampment of the Black Watch Regiment here: they kept their armoured vehicles on the green, and had their canteen in the village hall.

WETHERSFIELD
The Green c1965
W192011

The long white building has its roots in the 15th century. It was once The Red Lion, but later became a garage. There used to be a shed at the back where you could get your radio accumulator recharged, when radios had such things. During the Great War, The Lion served as a hospital.

WETHERSFIELD
High Street c1965
W192003

The now-demolished barn in the foreground was the premises of Wicks Contractors, land developers, builders and undertakers. The Wicks family also owned the 17th-century Briar Cottage, next door. The tenements with the crowstepped gable beyond were built as almshouses. They are now minus their veranda.

WETHERSFIELD, *The Dog Inn c1965* W192004

This driveway leads past the church to Wethersfield Hall. The village doctor once had his surgery at the Hall, though his patients disliked passing the graveyard whenever they visited him. Today, the ivy has really taken hold of the gate-piers. The Dog is still open for business, but not, one suspects, to many Hillman Imps.

GREAT BARDFIELD, *High Street c1965* G93013

Great Bardfield is a village that bills itself as a town. Its 17th-century Town House, on the left, was once a sort of part-time guildhall. The garage opposite has reverted to domestic duties, but Hitchcock's (where the lorry is) is still a thriving concern - part grocer's, part post office. The Brick House, beside it, used to be a fur factory.

GREAT BARDFIELD
High Street 1903 50566

Bardfield has a wealth of old buildings: the house on the left is 15th-century, as is Gobions - the distant white house. The village was once famous for its fair, where horses were bought and sold, and the 'trashy articles displayed on the hoopla stalls flashed under the naphtha flares like the crown jewels', as one witness poetically put it.

71

GREAT BARDFIELD, *Brook Street and the Memorial c1965* G93004

Great Bardfield's central green - the area on the left - has been heavily built upon. A Friends' Meeting House was erected there in 1804: the tree-shaded wall on the left surrounds its graveyard. At that time, Great Bardfield Hall was owned by a Quaker family - the Smiths - who were great benefactors to the parish.

GREAT BARDFIELD, *Brook Street c1965* G93008

The White Hart (right) is a 15th-century building with later additions. The thatched roof at the left-hand road junction belongs to Serjeant Bendlowes's Cottage. Bendlowes held various official posts under the Tudor monarchs, some of whom had to turn a blind eye to his Catholicism. The Cottage is one of several almshouses he endowed.

GREAT BARDFIELD
Brook Street 1903 50565

This fountain (left) was provided in 1860 by Henry Smith, who also built the Town Hall. It pumped water from a spring in Hall Meadows. The inhabitants were reluctant to forsake it when Bardfield acquired a mains water supply in the 1930s. Like The White Hart, The Three Horseshoes (right) is now an ex-pub.

GREAT BARDFIELD, *The Parish Church of St Mary the Virgin 1903* 50567

Nicknamed 'the Clock with the Church on It', because of the huge timepiece now on the other side of the tower, St Mary's dates from the 12th century. Its elevated site, however, suggests a place of pre-Christian worship. The gravestones in this photo are still in situ, though the railed plot (right) has been swamped by a holly tree.

GREAT BARDFIELD
Gibraltar Mill c1965
G93010

For many years, this octagonal windmill was in the hands of the influential Smith family, who also owned the nearby watermill. Built in c1660, it was converted into a house in 1957. The British acquisition of Gibraltar was a cause célèbre when the mill was still quite new. Could that be the reasoning behind its odd name?

GREAT SAMPFORD
Church Corner c1955 G91006

This row of cottages started life as one 15th-century house of the hall-and-wings type. It is now all one house again. St Michael's Church is mainly early 14th-century. In 1759 a Thaxted curate wrote that 'the church of Sampford does not look like a house of prayer, nor its vicar like a man of God.'

GREAT SAMPFORD
Moor End c1955
G91010

Like so many pubs, The White Horse has mutated into a house. The thatched cottage next door was once the home of the local carpenter, William Gray. He made coffins, amongst other things, and had his own standing ready in the kitchen. The house is still called Carpenters. A windmill used to stand across the road, behind the hedge.

GREAT SAMPFORD
The View from the Bridge c1955 G91007

Behind us is the bridge across the young River Pant. As recently as the early 1900s, it could still only carry horses - not carts. In times of flood it was impassable, and even the horses had to go by another route, three miles out of their way. In 1909 it was rebuilt by the County Council. The shop in the picture is now a house called the Store House.

DEBDEN
The Crossroads c1955
D89002

This was The Fox, one of five hostelries serving Debden in the 1950s. The area to the right is the edge of Debden Park - the grounds of Debden Hall that were landscaped in the late 18th century, possibly by the mighty Humphrey Repton. The Hall itself was demolished in 1935.

THE SURROUNDING VILLAGES: SOUTH

TAKELEY

The Four Ashes and the Shops c1965 T109002

Takeley was granted a market is 1253. It is essentially a thoroughfare village running along Stane Street (which does not look especially busy in this shot). The road is currently being bypassed by a dual carriageway that will whisk traffic to Takeley's neighbour, Stansted Airport. The village's railway station closed to passengers in 1952.

TAKELEY, *The Clock House c1965* T109005

Constructed c1600, this was probably a yeoman farmer's house associated with the Hallingbury Park estate. It was later split into two cottages, one of which was the local police house. The whole property was restored in the1960s. The clock itself is a one-handed 18th-century model, and has been a useful village timekeeper.

TAKELEY
Bamber's Green c1960
T109012

'Bamber's Green - Twinned with Heathrow Airport' has been the recent slogan here. What this means is that if Stansted's second runway gets the go-ahead, this hamlet will be obliterated. Bury Villas, seen here, will go. Quite what William Bennebury would have thought is anyone's guess: he was the 15th-century landowner whose name slurred into Bamber.

GREAT EASTON
The Swan c1960 G95006

Though considerably altered over the centuries, the Swan retains traces of 15th-century woodwork. In the 1930s, the landlord's son operated a taxi service from the pub, and sold petrol. After the War, he established a proper garage - Brown's - in the village. The car here is a pre-1956 Morris Traveller with a divided windscreen.

GREAT EASTON
The Endway c1960 G95008

The church is basically Norman. It gained its whimsical bell-tower in 1928. There is a stone, now set into the churchyard wall, reading: *'Near this spot lies a murdered man / Whose remains were found in Handless Spring. / Unfold the murderous deed if you can / And the wretch or wretches to justice bring.'* It dates from the 1830s.

GREAT EASTON
The Ford 1951 G95001

This is the River Chelmer. Within fifteen years of this photo, the roadway had been made into a proper bridge, and there had been an infilling of bungalows on the left-hand side. The horses serve to remind us of the agricultural nature of these villages: Great Easton was entirely engaged in growing cereal crops and soft fruits.

FELSTED
The Guildhall c1960
F76007

Felsted's Guildhall, like Finchingfield's, was built to accommodate the Trinity Guild. In 1564 it was taken over by Lord Riche as a schoolroom. This was the start of the famous Felsted School, which rose to the height of its fame in the 19th century under its headmaster W S Grignon. A new schoolhouse was built 1799-1801.

FELSTED, *The Mill c1960* F76015

Felsted had two watermills at the time of the Domesday survey, and it is likely that Felsted Mill and Hartford End Mill are on the same two sites. The current building here dates from 1858, its predecessor having burned down. It is now a house, though it had continued working until 1960, grinding wholemeal for a Chelmsford health-food company.

STEBBING
High Street c1960 S282014

The children's clothing and the 1950s Ford make this a real period piece. Stebbing, strung out along a mile-long road, has a fine collection of old buildings: the house with the leaning frontage is late 15th-century, the other cottages slightly later. At the top of the road is Burleton's store.

GREAT SALING
*St James' Church
1903* 50564

This is the manorial
core of Saling: the
church and the Hall.
St James' was built in
the 12th century, but
its earlier details have
been obscured by
later work. The Hall is
a 17th-century
extravaganza in red
and blue brick, with
curvilinear gables. It
contains some fine
oak panelling.

PANFIELD
The Hall 1906 55543

Panfield is a small village
with no real focal point.
The Hall occasionally
throws open its farmyard
and barns to host the
village fête. The building
is ascribed to c1500,
though successive lords
of the manor added new
wings, marked with their
initials and armorial
bearings. They removed
old wings too: the Hall
once extended further to
the right.

PANFIELD, *The Church of St Mary and St Christopher 1906* 55542

This mid-15th-century church was Victorianised in 1858. The lovely timber porch was left relatively untouched, however; and a grave-slab from an earlier church has recently been discovered beneath the pews. The rectory burned down in the 1950s. It was a Tudor building inside a later shell: those chimney-stacks betray its true vintage.

SHALFORD
St Andrew's Church 1909 62123

Shalford is the 'shallow ford' across the Pant. St Andrew's, standing by the river, is an early 14th-century church noted for its heraldic stained glass, and a peculiar trio of tomb recesses inside. Straw plaiting was an intensive cottage industry in Shalford in the 19th century: examples of it were even used to decorate the altar.

SHALFORD, *Braintree Road 1909* 62121

The cottages on the right were almshouses. They are gone now.
The white house just past them is known as the Penthouse - a
name connected with the fact that the village pound (or 'pent')
for stray cattle once stood here. In the street, the nanny is
pushing a pram of an unusual penny-farthing design.

INDEX

NAMES OF SUBSCRIBERS

The following people have kindly supported this book by subscribing to copies before publication.

Mrs N. E. Archer
Norman & Hazel Barker, Dunmow
Linda, David & Kevin Barry, Great Dunmow
Mr B. G. & Mrs S. E. Bassett, Thaxted
The Bell Family, Barnston
David Roger Bemment
Mark & Heather Brock, Thaxted
Dolly Brook & Family, Great Dunmow
Mrs D. Brooker, Little Easton, Dunmow
Mr & Mrs R. J. C. Brooker, Great Dunmow
J. M. D. Brown, C. J. Brown, B. A. Brown, Stebbing
Mr W. T. Buck & Mrs. M. J. E. Buck, Dunmow
Angela & Peter Canham, Derwent House
The Caton Family, Thaxted
The Chapman Family of Dunmow
The Clark Family, Stebbing
The Clarke Family, New Zealand
Mr G. W. Coe & Mrs V. J. Coe, Thaxted
Jane Copeman
Mr N. S. & Mrs M. E. Danford, Thaxted
Winifred Jessie Devoil
Mrs S. Dormer
Mr M. J. P. & Mrs E. A Downes
Gloria & Harry Ellis, Shalford
Robin & Jacqueline Farrant
Mr B. C. & Mrs M. E. Fairweather, Dunmow
Richard Foot & Margaret Rufus, Bran End, Stebbing
Mr P. & Mrs K. Frost & Family, Dunmow
Robert Arthur James Giles
C. Gobetti, Little Bardfield
Brian W. T. Goodey, Dunmow
Mr J. A. & Mrs. J. R. Gowers, Thaxted
The Gravelle Family, Dunmow
Mrs E. Hinton
George C. Huggett
The Jervis Family, Finchingfield
Mr P. G. & Mrs J. Jervis

Mary & Andrew Jensen, Barnston
Lynda Marsh
Mrs J. Marshall, Worle, Somerset
George & Doreen Mason, Dunmow
Graham Mellows, Great Easton
Linda Metson & Derek Ward, Barnston
P. H. F. Milne, Dunmow
The Moore Family, Great Dunmow
Robin N. Morgan, Thaxted
Mr Colin Morrison, Ongar, from Jo & John
Sidney & Molly Mottram, Takeley
Micheal G. O'Connell, Dunmow
Pat & Eddie Parslow, Dunmow
The Perry Family, Felsted
Mark Phillipson 2004
Ralph Pickford, Dunmow
The Powell-Allen Family, Barnston
Reverend I. M & Mrs E. R. Reed, Thaxted
Mr & Mrs Reynolds, Great Dunmow
Frederick C. Rivett, Dunmow
Richard & Gillian Robertson, Felsted, 2004
The Sandlin Family
Roger & Gwyneth Sell, Finchingfield
P. A. Serlin, C. R. Serlin and Spike, Thaxted
Rev. J. H. Shead
Keith & Ann Smith, Dunmow
Mr G. J. & Mrs. E. J. Squirrell, Barnston
Mr & Mrs M. Stokes, Thaxted
Douglas Suckling
Mrs A. S. Tee
Memories of Dunmow and Thaxted, R. & B. Townsend
William Tracey, Church End, Great Dunmow
Brenda Ann Verley, Great Dunmow
Phyllis & Herbert Verley, Germany
Walpole Family
Phyllis Ward, Great Dunmow
D. R. Warden
Bronte & Albie Wardle, Thaxted
Mr C. J. E. & Mrs S. L. Weet, Thaxted
John & Teresa Welsh, Dunmow
Arthur W. Whitehead, Dunmow
Richard & Grace Wilcox, Dunmow
Mike & Mandy Williams, Takeley, Essex
Mr W. T. & Mrs A. Wilson, Wethersfield
Jeremy, Jill and Rosie Woolcock

FRITH PRODUCTS & SERVICES

Francis Frith would doubtless be pleased to know that the pioneering publishing venture he started in 1860 still continues today. Over a hundred and forty years later, The Francis Frith Collection continues in the same innovative tradition and is now one of the foremost publishers of vintage photographs in the world. Some of the current activities include:

Interior Decoration

Today Frith's photographs can be seen framed and as giant wall murals in thousands of pubs, restaurants, hotels, banks, retail stores and other public buildings throughout the country. In every case they enhance the unique local atmosphere of the places they depict and provide reminders of gentler days in an increasingly busy and frenetic world.

Product Promotions

Frith products are used by many major companies to promote the sales of their own products or to reinforce their own history and heritage. Frith promotions have been used by Hovis bread, Courage beers, Scots Porage Oats, Colman's mustard, Cadbury's foods, Mellow Birds coffee, Dunhill pipe tobacco, Guinness, and Bulmer's Cider.

Genealogy and Family History

As the interest in family history and roots grows world-wide, more and more people are turning to Frith's photographs of Great Britain for images of the towns, villages and streets where their ancestors lived; and, of course, photographs of the churches and chapels where their ancestors were christened, married and buried are an essential part of every genealogy tree and family album.

Frith Products

All Frith photographs are available Framed or just as Mounted Prints and Posters (size 23 x 16 inches). These may be ordered from the address below. From time to time other products - Address Books, Calendars, Table Mats, etc - are available.

The Internet

Already fifty thousand Frith photographs can be viewed and purchased on the internet through the Frith websites and a myriad of partner sites.

For more detailed information on Frith companies and products, look at these sites:

www.francisfrith.co.uk
www.francisfrith.com
(for North American visitors)

See the complete list of Frith Books at:
www.francisfrith.co.uk
This web site is regularly updated with the latest list of publications from the Frith Book Company. If you wish to buy books relating to another part of the country that your local bookshop does not stock, you may purchase on-line.

For further information, trade, or author enquiries please contact us at the address below:
The Francis Frith Collection, Frith's Barn, Teffont, Salisbury, Wiltshire, England SP3 5QP.
Tel: +44 (0)1722 716 376 Fax: +44 (0)1722 716 881 Email: sales@francisfrith.co.uk

See Frith books on the internet at www.francisfrith.co.uk

FREE MOUNTED PRINT

Mounted Print
Overall size 14 x 11 inches

Fill in and cut out this voucher and return
it with your remittance for £2.25 (to cover postage and handling). Offer valid for delivery to UK addresses only.

Choose any photograph included in this book.
Your SEPIA print will be A4 in size. It will be mounted in a cream mount with a burgundy rule line (overall size 14 x 11 inches).

**Order additional Mounted Prints
at HALF PRICE (only £7.49 each*)**
If you would like to order more Frith prints from this book, possibly as gifts for friends and family, you can buy them at half price (with no additional postage and handling costs).

Have your Mounted Prints framed
For an extra £14.95 per print* you can have your mounted print(s) framed in an elegant polished wood and gilt moulding, overall size 16 x 13 inches (no additional postage and handling required).

---

* IMPORTANT!

These special prices are only available if you order at the same time as you order your free mounted print. You must use the ORIGINAL VOUCHER on this page (no copies permitted). We can only despatch to one address.

Send completed Voucher form to:
The Francis Frith Collection, Frith's Barn, Teffont, Salisbury, Wiltshire SP3 5QP

Voucher for **FREE** and Reduced Price Frith Prints

Please do not photocopy this voucher. Only the original is valid, so please fill it in, cut it out and return it to us with your order.

Picture ref no	Page no	Qty	Mounted @ £7.49	Framed + £14.95	Total Cost
		1	Free of charge*	£	£
			£7.49	£	£
			£7.49	£	£
			£7.49	£	£
			£7.49	£	£
			£7.49	£	£
Please allow 28 days for delivery			* Post & handling (UK)		£2.25
			Total Order Cost		£

Title of this book . . . .

I enclose a cheque/postal order for £ . . . .
made payable to 'The Francis Frith Collection'

OR please debit my Mastercard / Visa / Switch / Amex card
(credit cards please on all overseas orders), details below

Card Number

Issue No (Switch only)   Valid from (Amex/Switch)

Expires   Signature

Name Mr/Mrs/Ms ....

Address ....

....

....

.... Postcode ....

Daytime Tel No ....

Email ....

Valid to 31/12/05

Would you like to find out more about Francis Frith?

We have recently recruited some entertaining speakers who are happy to visit local groups, clubs and societies to give an illustrated talk documenting Frith's travels and photographs. If you are a member of such a group and are interested in hosting a presentation, we would love to hear from you.

Our speakers bring with them a small selection of our local town and county books, together with sample prints. They are happy to take orders. A small proportion of the order value is donated to the group who have hosted the presentation. The talks are therefore an excellent way of fundraising for small groups and societies.

Can you help us with information about any of the Frith photographs in this book?

We are gradually compiling an historical record for each of the photographs in the Frith archive. It is always fascinating to find out the names of the people shown in the pictures, as well as insights into the shops, buildings and other features depicted.

If you recognize anyone in the photographs in this book, or if you have information not already included in the author's caption, do let us know. We would love to hear from you, and will try to publish it in future books or articles.

Our production team

Frith books are produced by a small dedicated team at offices in the converted Grade II listed 18th-century barn at Teffont near Salisbury, illustrated above. Most have worked with the Frith Collection for many years. All have in common one quality: they have a passion for the Frith Collection. The team is constantly expanding, but currently includes:

Jason Buck, John Buck, Ruth Butler, Heather Crisp, David Davies, Isobel Hall, Julian Hight, Peter Horne, James Kinnear, Karen Kinnear, Tina Leary, Stuart Login, Amanda Lowe, David Marsh, Sue Molloy, Kate Rotondetto, Dean Scource, Eliza Sackett, Terence Sackett, Sandra Sampson, Adrian Sanders, Sandra Sanger, Julia Skinner, Claire Tarrier, Lewis Taylor, Shelley Tolcher and Lorraine Tuck.